Mathias Braschler
Madison Avenue

Mathias Braschler
Madison Avenue

Andreas Züst Verlag

Madison Avenue
America's Urban Sine Curve

For Donald Trump, the kitschy tycoon, it is the «best location in the world.» José Robaino, a black security officer from Harlem, hates the straight boulevard, «because everyone here kills himself right away.» Nowhere does a square foot of real estate cost more, not even in Hong Kong. Expensive lives are insured by the white-shirted officers of Met Life, the gigantic insurance company, whose baroque headquarters dominate the southern end of Madison Avenue. A scant four-and-a-half miles further north, almost at the end of this long street, the St. Helena Funeral Home takes care of corpses, mostly of obscure Hispanics. Old, banged-up Fords and Chryslers dodge through deep potholes in the streets around the derelict apartment blocks. Further down, at the level of Central Park, German luxury automobiles hum across the smoothest blacktop. People are high on cocaine and crack — but in geographically diverse places. New York City's Madison Avenue. The most expensive street in the world, cutting an excessively wide swathe through the island of Manhattan. It starts at faceless 23rd Street, fights its way up through busy Midtown and the successful Upper East Side, until it reaches the top in Harlem where business has been slow for decades now. Here, some blacks live in tin shacks. This is where the Swiss photographer, Mathias Braschler, spent eight months taking pictures in 1998. Not of the Avenue, not of the typical street scene with its yellow cabs or sophisticated New York ladies — this has long been an obnoxious cliché of American popular culture. No, he portrays people, simply, intimately: women, men, children, old people — some 85 in all.

It is a daring venture, whose grid of precision and seemingly monotonous uniformity informs each image with a surprising uniqueness. It is perhaps precisely because of the serial nature of Braschler's work and because he uses great depth of field, usually selecting the same focus that the huge differences become clear. His work shows us that the differences can nowhere be felt more keenly, more sharply, more clearly than in the seemingly same. The variety of uniformity.

He has created a blurred and complex, happy and sad reflection of urban America, a feverish sine curve of wealth and success as well as failure, of permanence and transitoriness, in short: of muddling through. An allegory of America at the end of the twentieth century, based on a reticent street on which the traffic runs from south to north, where no cinema, no theater distracts from real life. At the bottom, the middle-class; in the middle, the lower upper-class; further up, people wealthier than anywhere else; at the top, the very bottom, the ghetto, the substructure. It will be difficult to find harsher contrasts within such narrow confines. Often it is some thirty yards that separate different races or several million dollars of income. The famous American dream and its dreary reality — this is where they clash, mercilessly.

But Braschler's images do not only tell of this rather banal tension between two very familiar poles. Rather, he finds countless facets in-between. Rather than categorizing out of a preconceived notion or artificially forcing simple feelings, he achieves a reduction to that which is there. After all, that is all that really matters. Along the microcosm of Madison Avenue live

and work the descendants of immigrants, foreigners, white and protestant, black, Irish and Catholic, Caribbean, Pacific, South American, Jewish, Italian, Asian.

It isn't simply the poor and the wealthy, the have-nots and the plutocrats, but every conceivable class that can be found here. Despite the apparently massive social differences, the people portrayed by Braschler do share one thing: an enormous feeling of self-esteem, of pride to be here and now. No-one smiles, but everyone beams into the observing intruder's frontally positioned Hasselblad. This minimal difference is the source of the enormous power in Braschler's formally economical, black-and-white photographs. He captures the American Spirit, the continual hope that things will be good or at least better, the unbridled belief in oneself. Even though there is still a huge economic gap in the US at the turn of the millenium, Braschler nevertheless shows us an energetic nation of victors — both in the housing project and in the richly decorated penthouse apartment that only serves as a second home. Never is there any cynicism, because the photographer treats everyone with the same respect.

The homeless prostitute on crack, the overweight boxer, the underpaid dog-walker, the smart owner of an advertising agency, the black nanny of two white boys, the sly Mafia lawyer, the brunette working out at the gym, the banker with his bald pate imperfectly hidden under a few remnant strands of hair — their eyes are all sparkling. This is what they share, what connects them — the foundations of a strangely composed yet superficially fragmented country. Braschler, the European, came looking for contrasts, which of course he has found, but he has also found seemingly accidental points of contact. His picture of society is less a social study than a successful attempt at representing the melting pot, which has often been declared dead, in its absurd variations and bizarre convolutions. Braschler arrived in New York on a private project. He took pictures of Harlem girls at a special high-school for teenagers involved in early, and usually involuntary pregnancies. Of course, the future fathers have long abandoned their unborn children. This school is on Madison Avenue, a street which the young Swiss man believed to be splendid and glamorous and flawless throughout.

Instead of which he found bullet holes in the defaced walls of houses, boarded-up, paneless windows, longterm jobless people, a place that looked «like Beirut after the war.» It seemed that the war was still going on there, with rival gangs controlling the drug market, cheap crack mostly destroying the blacks, AIDS rampant; with homeless people rooting about trash cans for a piece of stale bread; a few blocks further south, the wealthy fighting to get richer still, at any cost; neighbours barely known to each other.

This street, its contrasts, captivated Braschler. He wanted to explore it with his camera, experience it from top to bottom. «This is my story.»

He abandoned his original idea of making a reportage, realizing that Madison Avenue would only be revealed to him by the people in the houses and behind the walls. His research took months. Many Harlemites thought that the bold white guy with his notepad was an undercover cop looking for incriminating material. The Italian fashion designers refused to talk to him, and so did the computer barons of IBM. But he did meet a prince and his princess, who proudly claimed never to have done a day's work in their whole lives, and he found a single black mother, who has never had any work.

Madison Avenue was named after James Madison, the very embodiment of the original American spirit. As one of the Founding Fathers, he participated in the drafting of the

American Constitution and of the Bill of Rights. While his father was a Virginia planter who kept slaves, he established the freedom of speech. He served as Secretary of State under President Thomas Jefferson, and was twice elected to the Presidency, in 1808 and 1812.

Sufficient reason, according to the wily New York city planners, to dedicate an avenue to him in his lifetime, even though it was not one of the city's grandest thoroughfares. On 30 April 1833, three years before James Madison died, the street bearing his name was officially entered into the street register. Because the two already established, splendid boulevards, Park and Fifth Avenue, were supposedly too far apart, the planners decided to insert a somewhat narrower parallel which initially stopped at 42nd Street. It was only in 1869 that it reached Harlem, a sparsely populated, white neighbourhood originally founded by the Dutch. In the nineteenth century, it was a cheaper alternative to Park Avenue for the upper middle-classes. It grew to its present length in the early twentieth century, when businesses and expensive hotels established themselves: the Ritz-Carlton, the Roosevelt, the Biltmore, as well as fashion stores selling the best European cloth, mostly for men. After the Second World War, advertising agencies moved in; the fashion industry followed suit, going where the avenue glitters most broadly: north of 42nd Street, it is 80 feet, but to the south of it a mere 70 feet wide. The architects built in the styles of Classicism, Modernism, Bauhaus, Art Deco; even a medieval-looking fortress was placed there. This odd in-betweenness of Madison Avenue can still be felt. Apart from the Whitney Museum of American Art, dedicated to twentieth-century American art and culture, none of the great New York attractions are on Madison Avenue. Walking along it, you can see the tip of the Empire State Building, the shrubs and trees of Central Park, the museums on Fifth, the magnificent homes on Park Avenue. Even the second Harlem Renaissance, which surprisingly started in the mid-1990s thanks to the economic boom, has not yet reached Madison. Instead of glittering highlights, it is dominated by austerity and a businesslike attitude. This, too, is America. Big and small business. And the old cliché, again and again, «Show me the money.»

For, of course, Madison Avenue stands for the material achievements of America at the close of the century. It is a reflection of the fun-loving consumer and entertainment society relentlessly powered by the Internet. The computer company, IBM, resides here as well as the Japanese entertainment giant, Sony. Everyday, the bankers of Credit Suisse First Boston at the Stock Exchange on Wall Street to the south shift billions of dollars, francs and yen around the world at the press of a few buttons. One of the world's largest advertising companies lavishes its products on the consumer and entertainment society; elegant galleries offer the most exquisite art. Patiently, a permanently fixed camera transmits its tremulous live images to a website. Also fashion, cosmetics, luxury. Gap. Armani. Versace. Yves Saint-Laurent. Revlon (President Clinton's lover was to work here). Peaches Goodwin, a kitchen maid at Mount Sinai Hospital in Spanish Harlem, whom Braschler photographed, sees none of this. She is happy if a day goes by without a prostitute getting beaten up, or anyone dying from an overdose or from alcohol poisoning.

Peter Hossli, born 1969 in Switzerland, has lived in New York since spring 1998. He is a freelance journalist.

Madison Avenue
Die urbane Sinuskurve Amerikas

Für Donald Trump, den superreichen New Yorker Baulöwen, ist es «die beste Lage der
Welt». José Robaino, ein schwarzer Sicherheitsbeamter aus Harlem, hasst den schnurge-
raden Boulevard, «weil sich hier alle sofort tot machen». Nirgends kostet der Quadratme-
ter Boden mehr, nicht mal in Hongkong. Am Hauptsitz des Versicherungsgiganten Met
Life, der ganz im Süden barock thront, versichern Angestellte in weissen Hemden Leben
für teures Geld. Knapp sieben Kilometer nördlich davon, am anderen Ende der langgezoge-
nen Strasse, bestattet das St. Helena Funeral Home Leichen von meist unbekannten
Hispanics. Dort fahren verbeulte Fords herum, durch tiefe Schlaglöcher, vorbei an verfal-
lenen Häuserblocks. Weiter südlich, auf der Höhe des Central Parks, brausen deutsche
Edelkarossen über ebenen Teer. Drogen findet man überall entlang der Strasse, ob Kokain
oder Crack hängt davon ab, wo man sich befindet.
Die Madison Avenue in New York City. Die teuerste Strasse der Welt. Wie eine übergrosse
Schneise durchdringt sie die Insel Manhattan. Sie fängt an der gesichtslosen 23. Strasse
an, rackert sich hoch durch die geschäftige Midtown, die geschäftüchtige Upper East
Side bis ganz hinauf nach Harlem, wo die Geschäfte seit Jahrzehnten miserabel laufen.
Teilweise leben Schwarze hier noch in Blechhütten. Dort hat der Schweizer Photograph
Mathias Braschler 1998 während acht Monaten photographiert. Nicht stimmige Stras-
senszenen mit senfgelben Taxen oder extravaganten New Yorkerinnen – all das ist längst
zum unerträglichen Klischee der amerikanischen Populärkultur verkommen. Nein, er
lichtet Menschen ab, macht schlichte und intime Porträts von Frauen, Männern, Kindern,
Alten, 85 an der Zahl.
Ein waghalsiges Unterfangen, dessen gerasterte Präzision und scheinbare Monotonie je-
dem Bild eine überraschende Einzigartigkeit verleiht. Gerade weil Braschler seriell arbeitet, stets eine grosse Tiefenschärfe und meist die gleichen frontalen Einstellungen wählt,
verdeutlicht er riesige Unterschiede. Die Vielfalt liegt in der Gleichförmigkeit. Entstanden
ist ein diffuses und komplexes, fröhliches und trauriges Bild des urbanen Amerika, eine
fiebrige Sinuskurve des Reichtums, des Erfolgs wie des Scheiterns, der Beständigkeit wie
der Vergänglichkeit. Eine Allegorie Amerikas am Ende des zwanzigsten Jahrhunderts am
Beispiel einer spröden Strasse, auf der der Verkehr von Süden nach Norden läuft, wo
weder ein Kino noch ein Theater vom wirklichen Leben ablenken. Unten mittelständisch, in
der Mitte untere Oberschicht, weiter oben so reich wie nirgends, ganz oben der tiefe Fall,
das Ghetto. Härtere Gegensätze auf kleinerem Raum gibt's kaum. Oft trennen an der
Madison Avenue weniger als 100 Meter Hautfarbe, Religion und etliche Millionen Dollar
Einkommen. Der famose amerikanische Traum und die klägliche Realität prallen hier
gnadenlos aufeinander.
Braschler findet zahlreiche Facetten zwischen Arm und Reich, Habenichtsen und Plutokra-
ten. Jede erdenkliche Klasse lebt hier. Trotz riesiger sozialer Unterschiede ist diesen Menschen eines gemein: das enorme Selbstwertgefühl, der gewaltige Stolz, gerade jetzt und
hier zu sein. Niemand lächelt, alle strahlen in die frontal gerichtete Hasselblad des beob-

achtenden Eindringlings. In diesem minimen Unterschied liegt die enorme Kraft von Braschlers formal einfachen schwarzweissen Fotos. Er fängt den American Spirit ein, diese stete Hoffnung, es werde dereinst gut oder zumindest besser, den unbändigen Glauben an sich selbst. Auch wenn die ökonomische Schere in den USA am Ausgang des Jahrtausends mehr denn je auseinanderklafft, so schildert Braschler eine Nation von lustvollen Siegern, in Housing Projects wie im reich dekorierten Penthouse-Apartment. Das wirkt darum nie zynisch, weil der Photograph allen mit demselben Respekt entgegentritt.

Die obdachlose und Crack-süchtige Prostituierte, der übergewichtige Boxer, der schlechtbezahlte Hundeausläufer, der smarte Werber, das schwarze Hausmädchen zweier weisser Buben, der verschlagene Mafiosi-Anwalt, die strampelnde Brünette im Fitnesssalon, der Bankier, der die Glatze mit den verbliebenen Strähnen zu verstecken sucht – ihre Augen funkeln. Braschler, der 1969 geborene Europäer, suchte auf der Madison Avenue nach Gegensätzen – und er fand Berührungspunkte. Sein Sozialgemälde ist daher weniger Milieustudie geworden als geglückter Versuch, den oft totgesagten Melting Pot in seiner absurden Vielfältigkeit und bizarren Verwicklung zu veranschaulichen.

Nach New York hat Braschler ursprünglich ein anderes Projekt geführt. In Harlem photographiert er Teenager, die viel zu früh und meist ungewollt schwanger wurden. Eine spezialisierte High School nimmt sich ihrer an. Sie liegt an der Madison Avenue, einer Strasse, von der der junge Schweizer stets dachte, sie sei prunkvoll, mondän und fleckenlos.

Jetzt findet er Einschusslöcher in verschmierten Häuserwänden, verbretterte Fenster ohne Scheiben, Langzeitarbeitslose, einen Ort, der «aussieht wie Beirut im Krieg». Rivalisierende Banden kontrollieren den Drogenhandel. Die Billigdroge Crack zerfrisst vor allem Schwarze. Aids wütet. Obdachlose durchwühlen Abfallkübel nach alten Broten. Wenige Blocks südlich davon kämpfen die Reichen um noch mehr Macht und Geld.

Diese Gegensätze packen Braschler. Von der ursprünglichen Idee, eine Reportage über die Strasse zu machen, kommt er ab. Erst die Menschen in den Häusern und hinter den Fassaden würden ihm die Madison Avenue wirklich offenbaren. Also macht er Porträts. Monatelang recherchiert Braschler. In Harlem denken viele, der kecke Weisse mit dem Notizblock und der Kamera sei ein getarnter Cop, der belastendes Material suche. Die italienischen Modedesigner zeigen ihm die kalte Schulter, genauso die Rechnerfürsten von IBM. Er trifft auf einen Prinzen und dessen Prinzessin, die stolz verkünden, nie in ihrem Leben gearbeitet zu haben, und auf eine alleinerziehende schwarze Mutter, die nie Arbeit hatte.

Benannt wurde die Madison Avenue nach James Madison, der wie nur wenige den ursprünglichen Geist der USA verkörpert. Als einer der Gründerväter schrieb er an der amerikanischen Verfassung und der Bill of Rights mit. Sein Vater hielt in Virginia noch Plantagensklaven, er trat für Redefreiheit ein. Unter Präsident Thomas Jefferson diente Madison als Aussenminister. 1808 und 1812 wählte ihn das Volk zum Präsidenten.

Für die Stadtplaner New Yorks Grund genug, ihm noch zu Lebzeiten eine Avenue zu widmen – wenn auch nicht die breiteste. Am 30. April 1833, drei Jahre vor Madisons Tod, wurde die nach ihm bezeichnete Strasse offiziell ins Bauregister eingetragen. Da die beiden bereits etablierten Prachtboulevards Park und Fifth Avenue angeblich zu weit auseinander lagen, entschied man sich, dazwischen eine etwas schmalere Parallele anzulegen. Sie reichte anfänglich bis zur 42. Strasse. Erst um 1869 erreichte sie das damals noch weisse Harlem. Im 19. Jahrhundert diente sie der oberen Mittelklasse hauptsächlich als günstigere Wohnalternative zur Park Avenue. Zu Beginn des 20. Jahrhunderts, die Strasse hatte ihre jetzige Länge erreicht, begannen sich Geschäfte und teure Hotels, wie das Ritz-Carlton, das Roosevelt oder das Biltmore niederzulassen. Erste Kleiderläden öffneten, sie führten feinste europäische Stoffe, jedoch fast ausschliesslich für Männer. Nach dem Zweiten Weltkrieg zogen Werbeagenturen ein. Es folgte die Modeindustrie. Sie zog dorthin, wo die Strasse am breitesten strahlt: Nördlich der 42. Strasse misst sie 24,4 Meter (80 Fuss) südlich bloss 21,4 Meter (70 Fuss). Architekten bauten im Stil des Klassizismus, Jugendstils, Bauhaus, Art Deco, sogar eine mittelalterlich anmutende Trutzburg wurde errichtet.

Noch heute ist die sonderbare Mittellage der Madison Avenue spürbar. Abgesehen vom Whitney Museum, das der amerikanischen Kultur des 20. Jahrhunderts huldigt, liegt keine der New Yorker Attraktionen an der Avenue. Wer ihr entlang flaniert, erblickt die Spitze des Empire State Buildings, die Büsche und Bäume des Central Parks, die Museen der Fifth, die Prunkhäuser an der Park Avenue. Selbst die zweite Harlem Renaissance, die Mitte der neunziger Jahre dank des Wirtschaftsbooms überraschend einsetzte, drang nie bis zur Madison vor. Statt schillernder Glanzpunkte dominieren allenorten kahle Nüchternheit und Geschäftsgebaren.

Die Madison Avenue steht für das, was Amerika am Ende des Jahrhunderts hervorgebracht hat. Sie ist ein Spiegelbild der lustvollen Konsum- und Entertainmentgesellschaft, deren rastloser Motor das Internet geworden ist. Der Computerhersteller IBM residiert hier, genau wie der japanische Unterhaltungsgigant Sony, die Banker von Credit Suisse First Boston verschieben per Knopfdruck täglich Milliarden Dollar, Franken und Yen an der südlich gelegenen Börse an der Wall Street. Eine der weltweit grössten Werbeagenturen berieselt die Spassgesellschaft, noble Galerien bieten erlesenste Kunst feil. Dann die Mode, die Kosmetik, der Luxus. Armani. Versace. Yves Saint-Laurent.

Von all dem bekommt Peaches Goodwin, eine von Braschler fotografierte Küchenangestellte im Mount Sinai Hospital in Spanish Harlem, nichts mit. Sie ist glücklich, wenn ein Tag ohne Drogentoten, Alkoholvergiftung oder verprügelte Prostituierte verstreicht.

Peter Hossli, 1969 in der Schweiz geboren, lebt seit Frühling 1998 in New York. Er arbeitet als freier Journalist.

Midtown 23rd - 60th Street

James Larosa
Lawyer specialized in white-
collar and organized crime cases.
26th Street

«I'm one of the most powerful lawyers in New York.»

Peter Murphy and David Intrador
Creative Directors at Young & Rubicam advertising agency.
40th Street

Peter: «The best thing about working on Madison: there is a bus line!»

Harold Grossmann

Gynecologist; studied in Berne, Switzerland.

30th Street

«I don't know which I love more, medicine or Switzerland.»

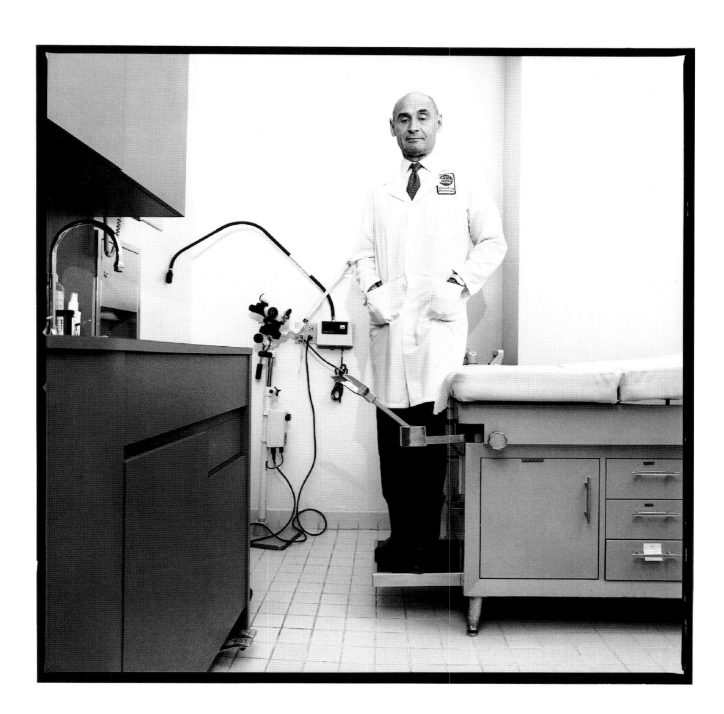

William Joyner
A homeless invalid who lost his leg in a shoot-out.
115th Street

«If I'm drunk, I'm an asshole. If I'm sober, I'm a great guy.»

Christine Gentile
Intermediate distance runner; working out at her gym.
54th Street

Bill Berkmann and Ingrid Michaels
Associate and manager of «The Associated» company,
with his personal assistant.
60th Street

Ingrid: «Madison is the epitome of what New York is all about.»

Urias Arias
Laborer at a carpet store; came to New York
from El Salvador three years ago.
34th Street

«I like New York very much, it's better than El Salvador.»

Al Perry
Lawyer.
24th Street

«Madison to me is fashion, advertising and beautiful people.»

Francis X. Gallogly
Pastor at St Patrick's Cathedral.
51st Street

«I love to preach. St Patrick's Cathedral is a very good place for it.»

Dominick Dunne
Freelance writer for «Vanity Fair».
45th Street

«To me, Madison is a glamorous avenue.»

Jennifer Clegg
Polo Jeans merchandiser from Texas.
58th Street

«I knew from a very young age on that I wanted to live in New York.»

Jack Hassanean, Mitch Platt and Silvester Murphy
Employees at «Reuben's Sandwich».
38th Street

Mitch: «I've been working here for too long.»

Takako Tsuij
A painter, at her own gallery.
58th Street

Eric Fox
Works in the finance department of a real-estate agency.
47th Street

«I take four smoke breaks a day.»

Eric B.Weimer
Insurance salesman.
37th Street

«I don't like to be together with people too much. I like to be by myself.»

Betsy Bentley Menna
Manager of «New York Public Library» on Madison Avenue.
35th Street

«The library means something to me, not the avenue.»

Jessica Feinsmith
Works at her father's real-estate agency.
29th Street

«Everybody says New York is so impersonal, but it is not for me down here at Madison Square Park.»

Matthew Buten
Investment banker.
53rd Street

«If I think of Madison, I think of where I get off the subway up to 86th Street. That's Madison Avenue to me, the identity of this avenue. It's about shopping and the arts.»

Heegu Yoon
Korean; has lived in New York since 1983;
owns a cleaner's.
27th Street

«Madison is good, because in this area there are no other cleaners.»

John Sacks
Design consultant; owner of a design agency.
23rd Street

«The nouveau riche designers are on Fifth Avenue. The high-end designers, the best ones, are on Madison.»

Dariusz Marczuk
Cleaner with Sony's. Came to New York from
Poland twelve years ago.
56th Street

Rodney Propp
Owner of a real-estate business.
62nd Street

«Madison is a wonderful place to do business.»

Carlo Blum Gentilomo
A Swiss who emigrated to New York 32 years ago.
36th Street

«Madison is the quintessence of New York.»

Hans Ulrich Doerig
Vice Chairman of the Executive Board and
Chief Risk Officer, Credit Suisse Group.
24th Street

Theresa Gallu and Patrick Trauzzi
Manager of the Bally shoe store, with his assistant.
59th Street

Patrick: «Madison is the pinnacle in retail shopping. That's where you want to be.»

Upper East Side 60th - 98th Street

Prince Robert Khimchiachvili and his wife
Helene von Hohenfriedenburg
The Prince is the 74th Grand Master of the Order of St. John.
63rd Street

«The kind of style, the kind of living that the upper class used to have here doesn't exist anymore.»

Eve de la Mothe Karoubi
Student at a private college.
91st Street

«The furthest I was up on Madison was 102nd Street.»

Gilles Mendel

Designer and co-owner of J. Mendel.
65th Street

«The price range of our articles is from $650 to $250,000.»

Martin G. Kolabas
Funeral Director.
82nd Street

«I work on Madison, but I don't make enough money to live on it.»

Michael F. Harris
Ex-dancer from Philadelphia; works for Barneys,
the elegant store, hailing cabs for customers.
61st Street

«I've seen nothing but the dark sides of New York since I came here.»

Dennis «Cowboy» Peabody
Collects bottles and scrap metal on Upper East Side.
61st Street

«I was married once. Not for all the money in the world I would do it again.»

Melton Magidson
Gallery owner.
80th Street

«I love this area.»

Erisa Yuki
Chief designer of «Yumi Katsura's».
71st Street

«I try not to be too Madison.»

Giorgio Nicholos and Nello Balan
The owner of «Nello's» restaurant, and his manager.
63rd Street

Giorgio: «Nello's is a high class restaurant. It's glamorous but still in a casual environment.»

Sean Johnson
Interior designer.
96th Street

«Most of my clients are young and wealthy New Yorkers who made their money on the stock market.»

Alexander R. Raydon
Gallery owner.
83rd Street

«For me it's not about having art. It's about knowing art, about loving art.»

Kathrine Merlo, Juliette Lang Cahn and Elise Pustilniic
Volunteers at the Whitney Museum of American Art.
75th Street

Elise: «Madison is elegant, but it dosen't have the individuality it used to have.»

Road workers
Laying down a new road surface during the night.
63rd Street

Donna Senko
Real-estate agent.
76th Street

«I'm an uptown girl. If I had a dog I would name it Madison.»

Michael Ress
Composer from Australia.
83rd Street

«I'm very close to the big breakthrough.»

Evett Whyte with Evan and Elias Wacht
Jamaican nanny with the children in her care.
87th Street

Evett: «I left Jamaica nine years ago for a better life.»

Suzanne Splan with Plume
Manager of Martino Midali Boutique, originally from Paris.
79th Street

«I always lived on Upper East Side.»

Leonida Zaloutskaya
Employee at an export business;
came to the US from Russia in 1991.
69th Street

«I only wear Versace. When Gianni Versace got killed, it was a nightmare for me.»

Ariel Meyerowitz, James Danziger,
Kate Palmer and Christina Bingel
James Danziger, owner of the renowned
Danziger Photo Gallery, with his employees.
71st Street

Lisa Shawn and Oliver
Mother and son on their way to his school.
78th Street

Lisa: «I grew up on Upper East Side. I've lived here all my life.»

Paulo Nascimento
Dogwalker from Brazil, came to New York one year ago.
94th Street

«With dogwalking I want to make money, to go back to Brazil and to have my own house.»

Herns Barthelemy
Doorman, immigrated from Haiti 24 years ago.
96th Street

«I don't like to be a doorman. It's not that I don't like the job. It's how you're getting treated!»

A. Laurance Kaiser IV
Owner of an exclusive real-estate agency.
63rd Street

«Madison has it all: culture, architecture and beauty, great shopping, wonderful restaurants and the most diverse group of dynamic people in the world.»

Alberto Tatti
Bartender, Italian, arrived in New York six months ago.
64th Street

Fred R. Anderson
Priest at the Madison Avenue Presbyterian Church.
74th Street

«This is one of the most prestigious and prominent churches in the USA.»

Peter Elliot
Owner and designer of Peter Elliot Boutique.
81st Street

«On Madison people have better taste and more money to spend.»

Harlem 98th - 138th Street

Antonio Lopez, Luz Diaz and Mike Lopez
Car spares salesmen.
129th Street

Debra Adams
Has been taking methadon for seven years;
HIV positive for nine years.
110th Street

«Drugs took five good years of my life away.»

John Santiago
Jobless.
104th Street

«When I was younger I did a lot of boxing. Now I wrestle more.»

Leroy Montgomery
Early retiree.
117th Street

Nicole, Regine and Keianna Noel
Single mother. Came to New York from Haiti as a child.
110th Street

«I don't really like it here. I like Brooklyn much better.»

Paula and Monthy Terry
A deeply religious couple.
117th Street

Willie Mae Whitted
Priest at the «Fountain of Living Waters Ministries» church.
119th Street

«1960 I came as a blues singer to New York. After one year I got saved and went to the church.»

King Musica, Anthony Rosa and King Blue Eyes
Anthony is a member of the Njeta-Gang, the other two
belong to the Gang of the Latin Kings. The three of
them have been in prison several times.
105th Street

King Musica: «I started selling drugs at 13. In my best times I made 10,000 $ a day. But I was 20 times
in prison... That's why I stopped now.»

Joseph Pagan
Vice Chairman of East Harlem.
115th Street

«One of the biggest problems we have in this neighbourhood is AIDS.»

Julius Vines
Invalid.
127th Street

«For me Madison isn't anything special; I'm just living here.»

Lourdes «Lulu» Velazquez
Drug runner, crack addict, homeless.
104th Street

«People in this area of Madison are full of shit.»

Israel Unger
Israeli truck driver; came to New York in 1983.
99th Street

«For me, Madison is just another street in New York.»

Russel «Fat Man» Field
Streetside vendor of fruit and potted plants.
128th Street

«I was working all my life on the streets — that's all I ever did.»

Nina Headen
Crack addict, currently living at a drug rehabilitation clinic.
128th Street

Rolando Hernandez
Cuban, immigrated to New York in 1980;
now owns a hairdressing salon.
117th Street

«Todavía no hablo inglés.» (I still don't speak English.)

Vincent Baber, Drew Jacobs and Herbert Brelend
Drew Jacobs, owner of a furniture store, with his employees.
128th Street

Drew: «Madison is part of my life. I come to work here every day.»

Gigi Lynette
Single mother; works for the Housing Authority.
105th Street

«I used to be a crackhead. I lost two jobs because of it.»

Raynard and Janai Smith
Policeman, with his daughter.
122nd Street

William Douglas Love II
Claims to be a professor at NYU.
129th Street

Ulysses Rogers
Crack addict, currently at a drug rehabilitation clinic.
128th Street

«I just want to live my life as a normal human being.»

Alexander Edwards
Dealt drugs for five years, but is no longer in this business.
107th Street

«I got shot three times, I cheated death three times... Madison or anywhere you go — the world is a ghetto.»

Peaches Goodwin
Works at the conveyor belt of the Mount Sinai Hospital kitchen.
99th Street

«Madison is a mixture of culture and people that you can get to know. All you have to do is to smile.»

Malik the Preacher
Blues singer; used to hang out in the drug scene
as a consumer and dealer.
109th Street

«This area isn't good. You can't have nice things and be around people that have nothing.»

Marry Hatcher and Teetee
Unemployed, with her granddaughter
131st Street

Brenda Robinson (Mrs. Bee)

Works at a fast food restaurant.
128th Street

«Momoney» (Malik Burns)
Rapper
110th Street

«When I was 18 all my friends were dead. Drug related... I try to leave Madison. It's a ghetto.»

Barbara
Crack addict.
135th Street

**My very special thanks to the following people,
without whose support this project would never have
seen the light of day:**
Marc Strebel, Adele Bachmann, Heidi and Alex
Braschler, Hedi Senteler, Carmen Sommerhalder,
Andreas Züst, and especially Monika Fischer.
**Ich möchte folgenden Personen, ohne deren Unter-
stützung diese Arbeit nie zustande gekommen wäre,
meinen ganz speziellen Dank ausdrücken:**
Marc Strebel, Adele Bachmann, Heidi und Alex
Braschler, Hedi Senteler, Carmen Sommerhalder,
Andreas Züst und insbesondere Monika Fischer.

A Hasselblad 2000 FCW with 50mm and 80mm lenses were used for this project which was
sponsored by Ilford, Hasselblad and Nikon.
Diese Arbeit wurde realisiert mit einer Hasselblad 2000 FCW mit einem 50mm und einem 80mm Objektiv.
Das Projekt wurde von den Firmen Ilford, Hasselblad und Nikon unterstützt.

Mathias Braschler — Madison Avenue

Design: Simone Eggstein, Zurich
Editing German: Miriam Wiesel, Berlin
Translation from the German: Margret Powell-Joss, Berne
Scans: Gert Schwab/Steidl, Schwab Scantechnik GbR, Göttingen
Printing: Steidl, Göttingen

© 1999 for the photographs: Mathias Braschler
© 1999 for the text: Peter Hossli
© for the map of Manhattan: Yale University Press
© 1999 for this edition: Andreas Züst Verlag
c/o Scalo Zurich—Berlin—New York
Head office: Weinbergstrasse 22a, CH-8001 Zurich/Switzerland,
phone +41-1-261 0910, fax +41-1-261 9262,
e-mail publishers@scalo.com, website www.scalo.com
Distributed in North America by D.A.P., New York City;
in Europe, Africa and Asia by Thames and Hudson, London;
in Germany, Austria and Switzerland by Scalo.

First Andreas Züst Edition 1999
ISBN 3-905328-16-X
Printed in Germany